Chasing Contentment

Freely Living Life through any Circumstance

Shayla Hilton

All Scripture quotations are taken from the King James Version (KJV) of the Holy Bible.

ISBN: 978-1-60383-516-9

Published by:
Holy Fire Publishing

www.ChristianPublish.com

Cover Design: Jay Cookingham

Printed in the United States of America and the United Kingdom

Dedication Page

To my mother and father (Bonita and Steve) and my entire family. I love you all!

To every woman who is determined to live the life God has uniquely designed for her to live. May God bless you greatly on your journey!

Contentment is refusing to
rush ahead of God.

Acknowledgments Page

All thanks and honor first belong to God who is truly the author of this book. Without God leading and directing my life I certainly would not be here today. I would like to thank my parents who are consistently there to love and support me. I am so grateful for and to those God has placed in my life to lead me, such as my Pastor, First Lady, Spiritual Parents, and other godly leaders. Your leadership and love mean the world to me. Also, to those who walk closely alongside me daily, praying for me, encouraging me, and holding me accountable; without you all, this would not be possible. Last, but certainly not least I would like to thank all of my family and friends who have journeyed with me at some point along the way. To each and every one of you I say thank you, I love you, and God bless you!

Contentment is trusting God
even after you have tried it
all.

Table of Contents

Contentment is found in intimacy with the Father, Son, and Holy Spirit.

Introduction

Are there people out there in the world actually living content lives? Do they know something that the rest of us do not know? Have you ever sat and wondered if contentment was truly possible or just some impossible, unattainable goal? I certainly have. If you have, then this book is for you. We hear a lot about contentment in our Christian communities, but what exactly is it? What is the big deal? Contentment is truly being satisfied or at ease in any situation. The question still remains, can this be a reality? I believe the answer is yes! You and I can experience contentment through every situation in life.

However, the problem is that today's woman is faced with so many of life's challenges on a daily basis. Who can even think about contentment when we are confronted with non-stop issues in our families, relationships, and careers? In the midst of everyday life, contentment can be the last thing on one's mind.

The average person is not just content by nature; he/she has to deliberately work at it. You see, contentment is a process. We have to decide that we are going to make it a reality in our own lives. We have to be determined to obtain it come what may. We have to chase contentment.

In the past, I spent many months, years even, of my own life living in discontentment. Never really happy with the seasons I was in. I was always uneasy and wishing that my life included whatever it was that I felt like I was missing at the time. I questioned if I would ever be satisfied with my life. I longed to learn the lessons that the Apostle Paul spoke about in Philippians 4:11 (KJV) not that I speak in respect of want: for I have learned, in whatsoever state I am, therewith to be content. Was this experience and kind of knowledge only available to Paul? I wondered if I too could one day say, "I have learned to be content". The truth is that I am still learning contentment—more and more every day.

In my journey, I have discovered that there are many things that keep us from contentment. I would like to share those things with you in the pages that follow of this book. This process requires a combination of things we put a stop to in our lives and new strategies that we must implement. We must take an authentic look into our own lives and accurately pinpoint the causes of our own discontentment. Please allow the Holy Spirit to reveal to you what changes need to be made. He wants to teach us, day by day, that our contentment is found in Christ and not the comforts of this world. It is my prayer that once you read this book, you will have the tools you need to not only chase contentment, but to conquer it and let it be evident in your life.

After applying these principles, your testimony will be, "I have learned to be content!"

Chapter One

Positively Powerful

It was an ordinary Saturday morning. Ah, it was so peaceful, and relaxing. I had no plans, nowhere to go, and nothing to do. Every once in a while, life will slow down just enough to get some rest. Have you ever had a Saturday like that? As I was waking up, I stretched my legs out, pulled the blankets back and with one eye slightly open, peeked at the clock. If it was too early, I was certainly going right back to sleep!

Lord, thank you for letting me live to see another day.

I turned the TV on, flipped through a few channels, and found nothing to watch. I lay there a little while longer to gather my thoughts and then decided to check Facebook to see what I might have missed. I scrolled for a few minutes, checked out the 'selfies', browsed a couple of articles, laughed at a few funny posts and then that was when I saw it.

"Hard times will always reveal true friends."

A friend I had not spoken to in a while had posted those exact words on her Facebook page. Is she talking about me? No, I whispered aloud, she could not possibly be talking about me. *We have not spoken in a while, BUT she obviously knows that I am her true friend, right?* I rationalized with myself.

Let me go to her page and see if she has said anything else. She is so mad at me…

Well, I did what any other curious woman would have done. Yes, you guessed it. I clicked on her profile picture and went directly to her page to see what else she had posted! Come on, you would have done the same thing, right? So, there I was on my perfectly peaceful Saturday morning, scrutinizing and over-analyzing everything on my friend's page. See, that was the moment where I wished I would have said a little prayer for peace and wisdom, but I didn't… Nope, I kept right on scrolling. Those little thoughts kept right on popping up and I kept right on listening to them. I am sure the devil was pleased with his sneaky, little work. After a few short seconds of strategic scrolling, I found exactly what I had been searching for. They say if you look hard enough eventually you will find something. I guess that is true. That was when I felt the second dagger.

"It's so ironic…the people in your life who say, 'I'm always going to be here for you' are the ones that walk away first."

See, she is accusing me of not being a good friend.

Who does she think she is?!

I felt myself getting angry. I was not sure why I was getting angry, but I knew one thing for sure, I was angry! In fact, I sat straight up in that bed, kicked that blanket all the way off, and put on my glasses for a closer look. Have you ever been mad, but you were not exactly sure what you were mad about which, in turn, made you even more upset because now you are all confused? That is where I was that day. So much for my peaceful morning. I wondered what I should say to her. How dare she talk badly about me on Facebook in front of all of our friends? I wondered what they thought about her little comments. Didn't she know I was busy? Didn't she know I had a life and had things going on too?

I should call her right now and tell her that I did not appreciate what she posted.

Call her right now.

SHE'S the one that is not a true friend.

You can probably guess what happened next. I got right out of Facebook, went to my favorites listed in my contacts, made a mental note to self to delete her from my favorites later on, and called. Ring. Ring. Ring. Ring. Why does the phone always seem like it rings forever when you really have something to say. I really was not even sure what I wanted to say, but I planned to improvise when I got her on the phone. The phone rang several times before going to her voicemail.

She is ignoring me…she does not want to talk to me…am I too late?

Was our friendship over forever?

Have you ever had one little 'spark' of a negative thought turn into a 'forest fire' in your mind? Man, it can happen so quickly! When I think back on that day, I am so glad that she did not answer that phone! Satan will do anything he can to cause confusion and create division. When I hung up, I was quickly convicted. I tried to explain to God that her post had hurt my feelings, that I had been offended, and that I always try to be a good friend to everyone. Our Heavenly Father was neither interested in me making excuses for my negative thoughts nor my jumping to conclusions. His attention was on my negative thinking. God spoke to me that morning about my thought life and the condition of my heart. Ouch!

God revealed to me that I had let the enemy slide negative thoughts into my mind and I did not have any facts. I did not even know if she was referring to me. That could have been directed toward someone else or no one at all. I truly did not know. Perhaps, she was talking about me; what was she going through though? Did she need some support? I knew we had not spoken in a while, I should have instantly thought to reach out and see how she was doing as opposed to getting so upset. I did not take the time to consider those things. I completely latched on to the first whisper from the enemy and ran with it. Has that ever happened to you? Please tell me that I am not the only one!

It was not long after that Saturday morning that I spoke with my friend again. After God pricked my heart, I decided to ignore those thoughts and feelings and take another approach. I did not bring up what I had been thinking or feeling, I simply asked how she had been doing. She just needed someone to talk to. It turned out she had been going through a lot and I was able to be a listening ear. She was very appreciative for our conversation. A perfectly good friendship could have been ruined as a result of nasty, negative thinking.

Do you ever find yourself thinking about the worst? Do you feel overwhelmed, consumed, or trapped by your thoughts? Do you see other people living positive and productive lives while you are struggling? Do you see your relationships being affected when those negative thoughts turn into words and slip out of your mouth?

Though it may seem impossible, all hope is not lost…

The truth is that negative thinking robs us of our contentment. One definition of content is satisfied with what one is or has; not wanting more or anything else. Why is contentment so important? Why should we chase it? John 16:33 (KJV) warns us *these things I have spoken unto you, that in me ye might have peace. In the world ye shall have tribulation: but be of good cheer; I have overcome the world.* It is inevitable; we are going to have troubles in this life. Remaining in Jesus and striving for contentment is our means of victorious living.

There are several subtle tricks that the enemy uses to keep us tangled up in discontentment. Before we even know it, we begin believing the lie that this is just who I am.

Another definition for contentment is ease of mind. With negative thoughts taking up so much space, there is certainly no ease of mind. A mind tormented by contradictory thoughts does not leave a person feeling content. One of the first issues we will tackle is negative thinking as we chase contentment. Who knew a thought could have such an effect on a person's life? I wonder how much more you and I could get done if our thoughts would just give us some rest?

A content mind is one that carefully filters every thought to determine its source.

If we are going to chase contentment we must take control; every thought must cooperate.

2 Corinthians 10:5 (KJV) says *casting down imaginations, and every high thing that exalteth itself against the knowledge of God, and bringing into captivity every thought to the obedience of Christ;* That sounds great and mighty powerful, but how do we bring every thought into captivity? It feels like those nasty, little thoughts hold us hostage; how do we break free and turn the tables?

While searching the Internet, I stumbled across the National Science Foundation's website where they reported that we [most people] have approximately 50,000 plus thoughts per day. Well, that seemed awfully discouraging to me! How in the world will we ever take all of those thoughts captive?! Do not feel defeated and give up; there are some practical things we can do.

As difficult as it is, we must be victorious, in this area, if we are ever going to effectively honor God with our lives. Thoughts are sly and subtle, but they have a significant impact. Therefore, we must determine the source of every thought that enters into our minds. When encountering our daily thoughts, there are at least three possible sources: God, Self, or Satan. You may be wondering, how can I decide who sent the thought and what should I do about it?

Sister, I pray that you are aware that we have an enemy. He hates us merely because we are chosen by God. He hates that we are so special to God and nothing can ever change that. Satan despises the fact that Jesus died on the Cross and redeemed us from our sins because of God's love for us. His only chance is to get us to walk away from God because God will never walk away from us. How does he go about trying to get us to walk away from God? By planting quiet, deceptive, little thoughts in our minds.

God does not love me.

I am such a sinner, I will never be forgiven.

Have you ever thought like that? If you are thinking something that contradicts God, His love, His goodness, or His promises, then it is simply not from Him. God is love and He would never have you or me thinking on negative, self-destructive thoughts. God will never go against His Word. Whenever we are still unsure, we can carefully check the Bible to see if the thought confirms or negates what is written. If what you are thinking twists biblical truths, those thoughts are most likely from Satan. Why would Satan put those thoughts into our minds? He is a liar, the truth is not in him, and he wants us to doubt God. Satan will always plot to get us away from God. Sound the alarm when there is any type of thought that leaves you feeling distant from God.

If Satan can convince God's girls to feel unloved, unworthy, and walk away from Our Creator then he thinks he has won. When we feel defeated and discouraged, trust that discontentment is close by.

Don't you worry though, contentment is up ahead…run from Satan's lies!

Satan is a manipulator and certainly to blame a lot of the time. However, dear sister, sometimes you and I are to blame. Our very own thoughts can get us into trouble.

I should get the promotion because I work harder than anyone else around here!

Who cares if they do not like it; I will do what makes me happy.

Have thoughts like those ever slipped into your mind? Sometimes thoughts benefit our flesh (selfish desires). At those moments we may not be considering others or more importantly, God's Will for our lives. We will discuss that in great detail in a later chapter. We may only consider what we want; what we feel is best for us. When things do not turn out the way we want, then we get upset. More often than not, we create those thoughts on our own. While these may not directly contradict God's Word, if we are not careful we can end up following these thoughts rather than following Jesus.

Instead of chasing hard after contentment, our disappointment could lead us to the dock of discontentment.

When self or Satan is the originator of thoughts in our minds, we must take them captive immediately!

How? What do we do?

First, we must acknowledge that it was not God who led us to think that way. When you catch yourself thinking like that, immediately remind yourself that it is not God. Why would a perfect, loving God ever cause havoc and confusion in our minds? God wants our minds free and clear. In fact, we are encouraged to have the mind of Christ!

Next, we must pray. It is imperative that we bind up those negative thoughts in the Name of Jesus while we loose peace and positivity in our minds. Matthew 18:18 (KJV) tells us *Verily I say unto you, Whatsoever ye shall bind on earth shall be bound in heaven: and whatsoever ye shall loose on earth shall be loosed in heaven.* We each have power and it is activated through prayer. Prayer will help you to discern and categorize each thought. Prayer will focus your mind and retrain your thinking. If you do not know what to pray or how to pray, begin by telling God that you are turning your thoughts over to Him. Ask Him to monitor each thought that you have in Jesus' Name.

You have the power (through Jesus) to change your mind about anything that should not be dwelling there. If thoughts of failure keep coming to mind, bind it up in the Name of Jesus and loose success over your life! When feelings of hate and anger try to slip into your mind, do not let them get comfortable there. Loose love and peace and embrace the change in your thinking.

Then, begin training your mind to think positive, truthful thoughts which can be found all throughout God's Word. It will not be easy to change the habits and patterns of your mind, but it can be done. You can retrain your mind to think about things differently. Once you begin thinking differently, your life will begin to reflect that which you have thought. It will be powerful to see what positive thinking can do. Friends, it is time to interrupt our patterns of thought! We must think on a different level if we are ever going to have everything that God said we can have. Philippians gives us an excellent example of what to think about.

Finally, brethren, whatsoever things are true, whatsoever things are honest, whatsoever things are just, whatsoever things are pure, whatsoever things are lovely, whatsoever things are of good report; if there be any virtue, and if there be any praise, think on these things. (Philippians 4:8 KJV).

A well-known television show host, shared an amazing story that helps us to see how we can change our thoughts even in devastating circumstances. In an article (I will paraphrase) but she reflected on a hard time in her life when she was recovering from a surgery, due to breast cancer, and dealing with divorce. She recounted that she went on a trip for work and on the plane home she sat next to a passenger who insisted on chatting. Up until this point, she had kept all she was dealing with private. He encouraged her to share her story because it would help others. That conversation helped her to think about what she was going through in a different way. We each have a 'passenger' listening attentively and encouraging us to think about things in a different way. That 'passenger' is the Holy Spirit. Will you listen as He works to get your thoughts on the right path?

Lastly, we have to destroy all of the strongholds. The enemy is so deceptive that he has planted some thoughts that reoccur and try to take up permanent space in our minds. Those are called strongholds and will not be taken captive as easily. However, God has given us the power to destroy strongholds (2 Corinthians 10:4). He has given us His mighty weapons, not worldly weapons to work with. There is no stronghold troubling you that God's power cannot destroy!

The interesting thing about strongholds is that they do not announce themselves as such. More than likely, you have no idea what you are even battling. You may have thought that way your entire life. Your mother and grandmother may have battled the same thoughts. It is not until God renews our minds that we are even aware that our thoughts are opposing the Will of God. As we destroy strongholds, we must fill our hearts and minds with God's truth. Any unoccupied space in our minds is room for the enemy to try and do his dirty work. We cannot play with negative thoughts because they cause even more trouble than we could ever think of. However, there is a remedy.

His truth terminates all contradictory thoughts.

The Bible has all of the answers you and I will ever need. God has His written truth available to us for all areas of our lives. You may need to think on truth pertaining to yourself, relationships, or family. Perhaps, you need God's truth to replace a negative thought about your career, spouse or His plan for your future. It is all there!

Finally, the third, but most important source, are thoughts that come from God. When thoughts come from Him they always align with His Word. When those God-thoughts arise in our minds, the response is simple: meditate on it. Think about godly thoughts day and night. The more we study God's Word, the better equipped we will be to determine if a thought is something that He would share with us or not. When we spend time with our Father we know His heart and character.

I am fearfully and wonderfully made.

I can do all things through Christ.

I am victorious!

Now, that is more like it! Those are God thoughts! That is the power we need! The more we think on thoughts from above, the more our minds will become Christ-like. As we resolve to take every thought captive, Christ will fill our minds and all the other thoughts have less and less space to occupy. Allowing our thoughts to run rampant will leave us discontented every day. Just as you would never leave the house without your body being covered, take the same precautions when it comes to your mind. Guard (cover) your mind with prayer. If we are going to get the victory over our thoughts, live a positively powerful life, and be content then we must pray daily for the covering of our minds. We will be tested over and over again, but we have what we need to pass the tests.

It was a pretty normal Tuesday except I had a different work assignment for that day. I got in my car, prepared for a longer commute, and drove to my destination. I pulled into the parking lot, turned my car off and took a deep breath. In just a few short minutes I would be standing in a room full of strangers. Strangers that all happened to be principals. Remember in elementary school when the thought of seeing the principal was terrifying? Take that feeling and multiple it by 30! There I was in a room full of principals and I was not one of them! I was an outsider.

You see, my principal could not make it to the principals' meeting that day; the assistant principal had to stay at the school to maintain order, so that left me to attend. Gulp. Sometimes, God will slide you into a situation so fast you do not even have time to process it. Don't you worry though, I had a plan. I was quietly going to slide in unnoticed, carefully slip onto the back row ever so gently, get the information, and creep back out. It seemed like a beautifully thought out plan, in my mind! Why doesn't a good plan ever work out? Well, I did manage to slide in quietly, but before I could even get situated in my seat the presented instructed the group to turn and share whatever it was that they were discussing with a neighbor. Oh, great! Seriously, what is this church or something? That was the moment when the thoughts popped up. Here we go again…

I do not belong here. They are all experienced. They are wondering why I am here. I will never fit in with this group.

I decided to handle this situation differently this time. I refused to allow negative thinking to defeat me once again. I knew I needed to give myself a spiritual pep talk. I was ready for those thoughts this time! I knew the source. Those were not God-thoughts so I bound them in the Name of Jesus. I started thinking about God's love and favor upon my life. I thought about God's plan for my life. I thought about the advantages of being His child. I thought about how the favor of God will take you places and your faith in God will keep you there. I chose not to be intimidated that day because God reminded me that if He lets me in a room, He will teach me how to maneuver it. I had to wing it a little bit, but I engaged in conversation with my principal neighbor that day. I shared what I was thinking based on my experiences and my school. As I changed my thinking that day, there was a positively powerful effect. I sat there contently, even 'out of place', with my mind at peace.

1. *Has negative thinking ever led you to make a decision that you later regretted?*

2. *How have negative thoughts affected your contentment?*

3. *What is one thing you can do today to change the way you think?*

Positive thinking is vital if you are going to live the life of contentment that God has planned for you. Begin by praying this prayer:

Heavenly Father,

I come today just to thank you and bless your holy name. You have been so good to me, and I can never thank you enough. Lord, I have been struggling with my thought-life and negative thinking is consuming me. All throughout the day, my mind swirls as the negativity tries to overtake me. I need your help. I cannot do it by myself. I need you to interrupt the patterns of negative thinking in my mind and destroy every stronghold that has been set up there. I believe that the Blood of Jesus will free my mind! As you remove every negative thought, replace it with a positive thought that shines the light on the truth of your Word. Teach me to mediate on your Word day and night. Teach me to only think and speak thoughts that come from you. As I chase hard after contentment, remind me that my thoughts are vital to the process. I thank you that even right now you are renewing my mind. I thank you that I will never think the same way again.

In Jesus' Most Powerful Name I pray, Amen.

Contentment is discerning the
Will of the Father for your
life.

Chapter Two

Ditching Doubt

Have you ever met a person full of faith? What stands out to you the most about his/her faith-life? If only we could all be as faith-filled! The opposite of a faith-filled life is a doubt-filled one. It is unfortunate that a lot of us probably fall into the second category. Have you ever felt like you were being chased down by doubt?

Some days doubt seems like your only constant companion. We, as godly women, want to walk through the door of faith, but doubt stands like a bodyguard in our way. Doubt is like a nasty, little weed growing alongside our faith; choking out our faith and limiting our vision for our lives. Don't we all want to live doubt-free lives in spite of our circumstances?

Doubt messes us up because it leaves us feeling depressed, hopeless, and faithless. We are inevitably left thinking that our lives will never get better and our situations will never change. Before you know it, you begin to believe the lie that nothing good ever happens to you.

Doubt keeps you from 'seeing' beyond your natural situation.

Do you remember the character Eeyore from the classic cartoon series, Winnie the Pooh? Eeyore, a close friend of Winnie the Pooh, always had a negative outlook on life. He always expected misfortune and had no hope of things improving. What a sad way to go through life. That poor, sad, depressed donkey always put himself down and never thought anything was good enough. Eeyore said things like, "nobody thinks of me…" and "I'll learn to live without it." While Eeyore is a fictional character, many of us can relate to his doubtful disposition. Have you ever had some Eeyore in you? I can admit that I have before. How do we free ourselves from 'club Eeyore' and change our outlook on life?

How do we ditch a doubtful and dreadful existence once and for all?

Confidently ditching doubt requires dismissing all traces of it from your mind immediately. How do we actually do that when the doubts just will not stop swirling? There are two things you can do right away: surround yourself with faith-filled people and steward your measure of faith.

Romans 10:17 (KJV) *so then faith cometh by hearing, and hearing by the word of God.* This verse remind us of how important it is to hear the Word of God in our day-to-day interactions. When we surround ourselves with faith-filled people, they just continually speak of God's goodness in a natural, unrehearsed way. Their whole conversation is different from that of doubt-filled individuals. Take a moment and think about the people you surround yourself with. Are they faith-filled people or doubt-filled people? If someone close to you was asked this question how would they answer when considering you?

Faith-filled people can shift a whole room with positivity and their trust in God! They simply just speak out what is in their hearts. The more you surround yourself with faith-filled people the better you will feel. You will begin to feel the faith coming back into your life! Who would have thought that your faith can increase just by hearing?! The more you are surrounded by faith-filled people the more you will start to speak faith-filled statements, without even realizing it! Things like, "I just believe God is going to make a way" will begin to spill right out of your mouth. That doubt will have no choice but to get out of there!

The other really important thing to do is steward your measure of faith. Romans 12:3 (KJV) says *for I say, through the grace given unto me, to every man that is among you, not to think of himself more highly than he ought to think; but to think soberly, according as God hath dealt to every man the measure of faith.* As you change your circle, and surround yourself with faith-filled people, do not compare your faith to theirs. Your faith should encourage one another not compete with one another. Their faith is different from yours just like your faith is different from mine. We each have been given measure of faith. God has given us the faith we need to accomplish His plans for our lives.

It is the responsibility of each of us to protect and pray over the faith given to us. We have to protect our measure of faith from doubt. We have to ask God to remove all of the doubt from our lives, so that we can fully function with our measure of faith.

Your measure of faith will allow you to trust that EVERYTHING is going to work out somehow through Christ Jesus; this guarantees a life of contentment. Doubt quickly rises up to challenge your measure of faith and questions whether EVERYTHING will truly work out or not.

How do we maintain our contentment? What does that look like?

A follower with firm faith refuses to be doubt-filled and tossed around by the friction of life. Instead, he/she is contently and securely fixed in place able to receive from the Father.

Have you ever sat at the beach and watched the ocean? The sights and sounds can be so peaceful and relaxing. If you have, you probably noticed the tossing of the waves. They are up then down; strong then subtle. Here one moment and then over there the next. Waves can be quite unpredictable. While most of us enjoy watching the waves, we must ensure that our lives do not follow the same pattern. Unaddressed doubt will shift us right into an unhealthy wave-like pattern.

We just cannot afford to be strong in our faith one moment and second guessing the next. As our Heavenly Father looks on, does He find "wave-like" faith in us? James 1:6 (KJV) says *but let him ask in faith, nothing wavering. For he that wavereth is like a wave of the sea driven with the wind and tossed.*

We say that God is a healer, but then secretly doubt if He really will heal. We believe God for a financial breakthrough, but then doubt when the creditors call. We plead with God on behalf of our lost family members, but shake our heads as we question if change is even possible for them. What is God to do with our wavering faith? Is He pleased?

Our scripture helps us to answer this question. Keeping James 1:6 in mind, verse 7 goes further to say, *such people should not expect to receive anything from the Lord.* Not Anything?! I think it is safe to say that our faith is very important to God. He wants us to be firm in our faith. Firm meaning securely fixed in place; not being tossed or thrown around. I believe that the word 'firm', used as an acronym, can help you and I remember to stand securely in faith through any situation.

The 'F' can remind us to focus. Whenever we begin to doubt, we can stop and focus on Jesus. When we really focus on Him, it is impossible to be tossed and driven by the waves of life. We have to be deliberate about calming our minds and determining what we will focus on. It is practically impossible to focus on Jesus and our doubts at the same time. We have to constantly remind ourselves that He is bigger than any situation we are facing.

The 'I' reminds us to inspect. When we start to experience the doubt, we should quickly inspect our hearts, minds, and speech. What thoughts are you thinking about your situation? What words are you speaking about your circumstances? Are your feelings overwhelming you? What we feel, think and say plays a vital role in our faith life. Do a quick inspection of your heart and mind right now. What thoughts and feelings have been taking precedence? We must change the thoughts and words that cause us to doubt. Quickly inspect the words that you have spoken today. Are your words feeding the doubt or extinguishing it? Only think and speak things that secure your faith.

The 'R' stands for recognize. We must recognize that the situation is short-term. I know it seems unbearable, but recognize it for what it is—temporary. It can be so difficult to see your way out of a situation when you are going through. You must keep yourself uplifted and know that you are coming out! Contentment is easier to access when you recognize that your situation will change and doubt cannot hold you!

Lastly, the 'M' stands for memory. If you and I are ever going to have firm faith and ditch the doubt, then we must tap into our memories and meditate on what God has done in the past. Memories are an amazing gift from God. Use it to your benefit! We can activate our faith and think about all that He has done for us. Is God a one-time God? Does His grace and power run out? Is there a limit on our blessings? Of course not! This alone will remind us of His goodness and power. Our memories help us to see who God is and what He is capable of. Hebrews 13:8 (KJV) states *Jesus Christ the same yesterday, and today, and forever.* If this is the case, then what is there to doubt? Will you make the decision to ditch doubt today?

▶ | ◀ Personal Reflection ▶ | ◀

1.   *Do you often find yourself struggling with doubt?*

2.   *What area(s) do you consistently doubt God in?*

3.   *What one thing can you do today to ditch doubt and regain your contentment?*

It is time to ditch doubt! If you are ready, begin by praying this prayer:

Heavenly Father,

I thank you that there are great plans in store for my life! I need your help because I struggle with doubt. Please forgive me because sometimes I even doubt you, Lord. Send faith-filled people into my life that I may journey with. Teach me to steward my measure of faith that you have given me. Day by day help me to live a content life firm in my faith. In Jesus' Name I pray, Amen.

We simply cannot force God to adhere to our timelines.

Chapter Three

From Distrust to Trust

Have your hopes, dreams, and desires ever been flying high in the sky like helium filled balloons only to be burst by the sharp 'pins' of life? In other words, have you ever been disappointed? I mean really, really disappointed. Not like disappointed when that cute dress is not in your size, or when someone whips into your parking spot at the grocery store. No! I am talking about disappointment that aches in your soul. You know, that disappointment that leaves you feeling just sick, defeated, and hopeless! You may have found yourself feeling emotional, confused, and unsettled without proper warning. It may seem like some people trust God more than you do. Some of God's girls are able to push past that deep disappointment and just trust God through anything.

I have an announcement to make. I am not that girl…I wish that I was.

In fact, I have had to work really hard at trusting Him. It does not really come that naturally to me, but I am getting better and better.

You may be thinking, can I trust God, or is my life every going to get better?

I have spent many days thinking that God had forgotten me. I wondered if God was still there, if I was being punished, or if things would ever change. I wondered if the negativity I perceived around me would ever get better. There was one time in particular that I was really challenged to trust God.

Yes! I was so excited! I was about to do something that I had waited my entire life to do.

Teach.

I was going to have my very own classroom with my very own students. I could just see it. My beautifully decorated room with colorful bulletin boards, neatly grouped desks, and sweet, perfect, little children who were all ready to learn.

Yes, Ms. Hilton, please teach us everything we need to know.

Well, there was one major problem with my little fantasy. No one was calling me to come teach in their school! What was the problem? You **do not** stand between a teacher and her bulletin boards! I had turned in my application and resume` to the district. Surely they had seen that I would be a great candidate, right? I thought everyone said there was such a huge need for teachers? *Well, here I am, pick me,* I thought. There I was feeling panicked and misled as I watched other people living their lives and excelling in their careers. It felt like a sick joke and I was on the outside of the funny.

The days and weeks continued to drag by and I still did not have a job. My excitement quickly turned to disappointment. Then, I even felt a little resentful. Maybe God did not want to be bothered with this type of thing. Maybe I needed to be more proactive and take control of this matter. Perhaps, I could not trust God to come through in this particular situation. What if, God did not want to be bothered with me? Those thoughts again! To make matters worse, my very best friend, who had graduated with me got a teaching job quickly and I still had not heard anything at all. I was so excited for her, but felt so sorry for myself. Unemployed and miserable party of one.

I knew exactly what I had to do…take matters into my own hands.

I created a list of all the possible elementary schools in the district. I began researching each school and contemplating if *I* would want to work there or not. I know what you are probably thinking; did you even pray and ask God to show you the school he wanted you to work in?

Well, no. I did not. I could figure this one out on my own, couldn't I? The answer turned out to be no.

Unfortunately, I did not trust that God was going to come through and I was leaning on my own understanding of the situation. It sure caused me a lot of unnecessary worry. I was a frazzled mess during that time! The bible instructs us in Proverbs 3:5-6 (KJV) *trust in the Lord with all thine heart; and lean not unto thine own understanding. In all thy ways acknowledge him, and he shall direct thy paths.* I must have missed that scripture somewhere along the way.

Have you ever been waiting on a change in your life and decided to move ahead of God because *you* felt like He was taking too long? Thankfully, when God had enough of me running around the city, like a crazy woman, with my school checklist, He put the right people in my path to lead me to the school He wanted me to work in. Interestingly enough, the school He led me to was not one of the ones at the top of my list. Had I yielded to my own understanding, I would have been in a school that God did not want me in. Sometimes, we just have to rest in Him and let trust flood our hearts.

Isn't it funny how God will close doors that He does not want us to walk through and open doors that He has available for us?

When we take a closer look at the scripture, we can see how it leads us past our distrust. The first part of the verse encourages us to trust in the Lord with all of our hearts. Now, let's just be honest, when you have been smacked in the face with disappointment, trusting in the Lord with all your heart is not the easiest thing to do. In fact, it is quite difficult! Before we know it, our hearts are full of distrust. We silently wonder, *am I really a Christian if I am struggling like this to trust God?* You may be wondering what distrust has to do with contentment. Well, you see, distrust is the root cause of discontentment.

While you may not have had a career disappointment such as I did, could it be that you struggle with your self-image, health or weight? We as women are constantly comparing ourselves, or being compared, to other women. How many times have you sat in the mirror analyzing everything that is bulging, hanging, sagging, or leaning? Can you trust God in those areas? God said that we are fearfully and wonderfully made (Psalm 139:14); begin by trusting that He made you just the way He wants you. The more we struggle with trust, the more we feel alone, isolate ourselves, and not trust anyone around us.

Will your heart allow you to trust and believe what He has already spoken?

What is it that causes us to believe what some people say, but not what others say? Why do we trust the promises of some, but not others? Often, it comes down to whether or not we have a relationship with the individual. We are always more likely to believe someone we know and trust. Could it mean that our relationship with God needs more intimacy when we struggle to trust Him?

We must get to the place where we believe EVERYTHING God says.

Think about the relationship you have with your best friend, spouse, parent, or child. If you have a close relationship with them then it is probably easy for you to trust what he/she says or does. Our relationship with God, through Jesus, is even more important than those relationships. We have to deliberately spend time with God, share with Him, listen to Him, and learn what is on His heart. As time goes by, you will just begin to believe what He says because you know His character. You will know in your heart that He can be trusted. This happens through prayer.

Prayer weeds out the distrust in your heart and plants seeds of trust. If you do not know what to pray, begin by asking God to remove all of the distrust from your heart. Tell Him that you are willing to trust, but you need His help in Jesus' Name. As you cultivate your relationship with Him, feel free to share with Him openly; that is how trust is built. Tell Him how tired you are of dealing with this situation. Tell Him that you feel ashamed for not trusting Him. He will not be angry with you. As you take time with Him trust will develop.

While God knows us completely, we have to get to know Him intimately.

Have you ever seen or heard someone being accused of a crime and/or inappropriate action? Someone that knows him/her well will often speak up and say that the person would never do something like that. What makes them so sure? They have built relationship with the individual and trust that they know the person's character. At times, people can fool us. You never have to worry about that with God. You can always trust what you know about Him.

Has God ever given you a Word of encouragement? Maybe the Word came through a scripture, a trusted person, or a whisper down in your spirit. Perhaps, you are struggling with a sickness or disease and you feel like God is going to heal you. You go to church and the preacher is preaching from Isaiah 53:5 (KJV) *...and with his stripes we are healed.* Then, a friend tells you that God said you were healed. Will you trust what you have received?

Well, how can you trust God when your body still aches, you see the physical effects of the sickness, and you hear the doctor's reports? How can you possibly be content with everything you are experiencing? Well, dear friend, there is only one thing you can do, and it sounds really strange.

You must completely ignore what your senses are suggesting.

2 Corinthians 5:7 (KJV) states *for we walk by faith, not by sight.* Walking by faith looks like trusting God in spite of what our senses are telling us. Keep trusting

God when what you see is confusing. Keep trusting God when what you hear is questionable. Keep trusting God when what you feel is misleading. This is such a difficult task because we live in this natural world and everything is based upon our senses. We, as God's children, must remember that we are not of this world, so we must be guided by the Holy Spirit. Just know that as you ignore your senses and are led by the Holy Spirit, you will look completely crazy to the world!

"Doesn't he know that he has cancer, why is he praising God?"

"What is she so happy about; didn't her husband just leave her?"

"Didn't their child just get arrested, why are they still going to church?"

"I thought she got passed over for that promotion, why is she thanking Jesus?"

People will talk. They will question you to your face and behind your back. That is alright. Do not worry about people. Just trust God and keep on looking crazy to them because He will most certainly come through for you! He is in relationship with you and would never leave you stranded.

God does not expect for us to go through all of this alone. He knows that learning to completely trust Him completely can be difficult. We have to acknowledge that we need His help. When we acknowledge that we need Him, He will come quickly to our rescue.

Our contentment is anchored in Christ when we acknowledge that we need help.

We are reminded that when we acknowledge Him, He will direct our paths (Proverbs 3:5-6). I do not know about you, but I need God to direct my path. Every time I have tried to direct my own path, I end up in a mess. Every single time; it never fails. No, I do not know where He will lead me, or how long it will take, but I just have to trust that it will be better than the mess I would lead myself into. In fact, it will be much better because He loves me so much. He loves you too!

It goes back to building relationship with Him. Think about the people that are nearest and dearest to you in life. Would you ever intentionally lead them the wrong way? Of course not! Why would our loving Heavenly Father do that to us? He would not. Just let Him direct you. Trust that He knows what He is doing. Trust that He has got you.

I read a beautiful story about a woman that was diagnosed with breast cancer in her early 30s. She was preparing to get married, but her doctor said she only had approximately six to nine months to live. She was encouraged to set her affairs in order. Well, she had two choices: she could believe what her senses were suggesting or she could trust God and fight. She chose the latter. She told the doctors that she was not going to die. She trusted God. The article shared that it had been seven years since that incident and the woman is still alive and cancer-free. She was courageous enough to trust God right in the face of her challenges.

Have you ever been to one of those team building retreats? You know, the ones where they get the whole team, group or organization together and head out into the woods. Before you know it, everyone is holding hands, walking across logs, or being blindfolded and led by a partner. They call these 'trust activities'. As you might have guessed, that is not exactly my idea of a good time, but I always go along with it for the sake of the team. Being one with nature is not really my thing, but I do think that there are some valuable insights to be gained from the activities.

You are put in various situations where you have no choice but to trust the people you are with. Then, there is the ultimate trust activity. That is the activity where one member of the group stands up on a log, facing away from the group. The remaining members of the team stand in two rows facing one another with hands interlocked tightly with the person standing across from him/her. The one individual standing on the log must fall backwards into the arms of the group members, trusting that they will catch him/her.

Keep in mind this person is not looking at the group, so they have idea if they will actually be caught or not. Imagine for a moment, if you will, that you are standing up on that log and instead of the people God is behind you with His arms outstretched. He is ready to catch you. Will you trust Him enough to just fall back into His arms?

1.   In which area(s) do you struggle to trust God?

2.   How has distrust affected your contentment?

3.   What step can you take today to begin trusting God?

If you are going to live the life of contentment that God has planned for you, trusting Him is a necessity. Begin by praying this prayer:

Heavenly Father,

I thank you for life. I thank you for desiring to have a relationship with me. Lord, I confess that I have not always trusted you. I have preferred to do things my own way. Please forgive me and change my heart. Help me to do my part in cultivating our relationship. Teach me to trust your heart and your character. Show me how to put my confidence in you. Lead me in walking by faith and not by sight. When distrust tries to sneak into my heart, block it quickly and fill that space with your love. I thank you in advance that trusting you is transforming my life, which helps me to be content with where I am. In Jesus' Name I pray, Amen.

*It was never God's intention
for us to live our lives
paralyzed by fear.*

Chapter Four

Courageous: Facing the Fear

Did you know that there were hundreds and hundreds of different phobias? We might be convinced that we all have some type of phobia looking at the lengthy lists found all over the Internet! I do not know about you, but I would rather not claim any of them! A phobia is defined as a persistent, irrational fear of a specific object, activity, or situation that leads to a compelling desire to avoid it. Considering that definition, now do you have any phobias? While you may not have a phobia per se, many of us deal with fear on a regular basis. Have you ever been crippled by fear? Often, we are faced with situational fear where a certain situation, event, or circumstance brings about fear. Some of God's women, with great potential, are being immobilized by fear daily.

The enemy uses fear to keep us from going after all that God has for us. When we are fearful, we will not charge forward and conquer the land! Fear leaves us feeling stuck, hopeless, and unsettled. If we are not able to take control of our thoughts and persistent panic, it can quickly turn into gripping fear.

It was never God's intention for us to live our lives paralyzed by fear.

Have you ever decided not to go after a dream because you were just too scared to try? Have you ever turned down the opportunity of a lifetime because you were not sure about the outcome? This chapter will challenge us to courageously stare fear in the face. As a result, the spirit of fear will be bound and we will be able to walk freely in contentment. Ultimately, we all want to live a full life without fear.

Fear tries to creep up on us in many different ways. Perhaps, you or someone you know is terrified of public speaking. What is it that makes the thought of talking in front of a group of people so traumatic? Just the thought of it may cause your heart to begin to race, you suddenly break out in a sweat, and your legs may begin to feel like Jell-O. You begin to think things like, I just can't do it or I'm not strong enough. Maybe that is not your fear, but you might have a fear of failure. You panic when you take on a new task or job because the thought of not succeeding is crushing to you. Feelings of defeat and embarrassment try to attack you before you even get started.

To avoid the possibility of failing, you avoid new opportunities which inevitably leave you performing beneath your potential.

You see, that is the problem with fear. Fear never allows for contentment. Fear keeps people trapped and too scared to move forward. Your flesh may even be comfortable with the fear. We can become accustomed to anything after a while. However, your spirit will never be satisfied because your spirit is aware that God has so much more for you. When your spirit is dissatisfied you can forget about being content. Fear will keep you from moving toward God's best.

What happens is that we end up seeing others who are embracing their God-given destinies. We see individuals who appear to be fearless! Is this truly a possibility?

When I think of individuals that seem to be fearless, I instantly think about firefighters. Maybe you have seen on television or in real-life these brave men and women quickly rush into flaming buildings. It is an amazing sight to see. Needless to say, firefighters are quite the opposite of fearful. In fact, they are extremely courageous! While everyone else is running away from dangerously burning buildings, they are running right in to handle the situation. Now, if that is not courage, then I do not know what is. These individuals willingly run into deadly situations every day to benefit others.

Is this to suggest that all firefighters are fearless people? Well, I do not know, but they are human, so I would suppose that they experience fear like the rest of us. Somehow they are able to feel the fear or uneasiness and still do what needs to be done. Is the same possible for you and I? Can we feel fear pressing in on us, and choose to move forward doing what needs to be done?

When searching the Bible for a courageous person, among many, Joshua stood out to me. However, I have often wondered was Joshua a man who struggled greatly with fear? Possibly, it was his situation that brought about great fear. Joshua had the task of actually leading God's people into the Promised Land. Now, that is a scary thought! Joshua had been in the wilderness along with everyone else, and served beside Moses. In fact, he led the army. He had seen first-hand Moses' struggles with the people. I can image Moses and Joshua giving each other the look as to say, "Here they go complaining again". He had an up close look at the frustrations and struggles of leadership as he watched Moses. I wonder did Joshua ever think to himself that he was glad he wasn't

Moses; who would want to deal with all of that mess. God used Moses to tell the people over and over again not to be afraid.

As the narrative goes, before the death of Moses, God told him that Joshua would be his successor (Deuteronomy 31:14). Imagine that type of pressure! Everyone knows that God used Moses mightily, how was anyone ever supposed to follow that? Don't forget all of the miracles! Do you think that is what Joshua was thinking? Better Joshua than I because I probably would have fainted. I do not know exactly how Joshua was feeling, but I suspect there was some fear there. God told him numerous times not to be afraid. If he was not fearful I cannot imagine God would have kept saying that. When God spoke to Joshua on several different occasions, the message was still consistent:

Only be thou strong and very courageous, that thou mayest observe to do according to all the law, which Moses my servant commanded thee: turn not from it to the right hand or to the left, that thou mayest prosper withersoever thou goest. (Joshua 1:7 KJV)

Have not I commanded thee? Be strong and of a good courage; be not afraid, neither be thou dismayed: for the LORD thy God is with thee whithersoever thou goest. (Joshua 1:9 KJV)

And the LORD said unto Joshua, Fear not, neither be thou dismayed: take all the people of war with thee, and arise, go up to Ai: see, I have given into thy hand the king of Ai, and his people, and his city, and his land: (Joshua 8:1 KJV)

And the LORD said unto Joshua, Fear them not: for I have delivered them into thine hand; there shall not a man of them stand before thee. (Joshua 10:8 KJV)

God wanted Joshua to release the fear and be courageous. Joshua was able to do it. I pray the same will be true for you and I. Has God shared with you that He wants to use you in a mighty way? What is a woman of God to do? Miss out on an opportunity to glorify Him or face the fear and just do it?

How do we follow Joshua's example and be courageous in spite of fear? When we are faced with fear, giving in to it and becoming stuck is not our best option.

Fighting fear requires forward action! Scripture tells us that faith without works is dead (James 2:17). Forward action entails three things: seek God, start moving, and then see victory. I believe it is practically impossible to think that we will never fear anything in life.

Unexpected things happen all of the time. Therefore, fear is to be expected. It is what we do with that fear that matters. We are encouraged with 2 Timothy 1:7 (KJV) which reads *for God hath not given us the spirit of fear; but of power, and of love, and of a sound mind.* We have to use what He did give us in conjunction with our own action if we are going to combat the fear.

We have to immediately seek God when we begin to fear. Joshua took the time to listen carefully to the instructions of the Lord. As we seek God, He will calm our souls and give us a strategy. He will tell you how to pray about the very thing you are fearing. He will tell you how to handle the fear before it has a chance to get you bound. Romans 8:15 (KJV) shares *for ye have not received the spirit of bondage again to fear; but ye have received the Spirit of adoption, whereby we cry, Abba, Father.* God did not give us the spirit of fear; He gave us a sound mind to think clearly and strategize.

The second step is that we must start moving. Whatever God instructs, just start moving in that direction. After speaking with God, Joshua started moving! He either went to the people to tell them what God said or he and the soldiers started moving to do as instructed. It may seem impossible, but just take one step in the direction He is leading. Remember, God did not give us the spirit of fear; He gave us love. If you really love and trust Him, then you will start moving. 1 John 4:18 (KJV) says *there is no fear in love; but perfect love casteth out fear: because fear hath torment. He that feareth is not made perfect in love.*

As a result of fighting the fear, we will see victory in our lives. After all, God did not give us the spirit of fear; He gave us power! That power comes from Him and brings about victory where there was once fear. Joshua was able to take possession of the land when he chose action over fear. He heard the Word of the Lord and responded with action.

I do not know what fear you are facing today. Only you and God know that. Should you go back to school, start a business, or write a book? Maybe you are supposed to change careers, reach out to some people, and/or start an interest group or bible study. If you have tried one of these things in the past, and it did not work out then you are probably dealing with the fear of failure. You may not want to try again, but I encourage you to seek God and start moving. You will never be able to live contently until you face the fear and live out your purpose.

▶ | ◀ Personal Reflection ▶ | ◀

1. *Do you feel like fear is holding you back from being who you are called to be?*

2. *If fear was not standing in your way what new things would you try?*

3. *What is one thing you can do today to combat fear and embrace contentment?*

Are you ready to courageously live a life of contentment? If so, begin by praying this prayer:

Heavenly Father,

I thank you that you created me to live courageously! Lord, forgive me because sometimes I allow fear to get in the way. Teach me that my contentment is in courageously living for you. Give me strength and courage to move forward even when I am fearful. I believe that your power will lead me into victory every time. In Jesus' Name I pray, Amen.

The most important thing to remember is that our contentment is found in Christ alone.

Chapter Five

Confidence is Calling

Have you ever heard phrases like 'green with envy' or 'green-eyed monster'? These phrases are often used in reference to someone who is a very jealous person. Why does she have that? How did she get that before I did? Someone green with envy might be overheard making comments like those. Certainly, none of us would ever own up to being a green-eyed monster, but we have all been jealous from time to time, right?

Jealousy will get into position like a defensive end and tackle your contentment to the ground faster than anything else. As women, we often compare ourselves to other women and that never seems to end well for us. Why do we keep doing that to ourselves? Before we know it, we are gloomy and have worked ourselves into an emotional fit due to jealousy. Meanwhile, the enemy is pleased with his work as we constantly sulk over our sad little lives, or so we perceive them to be. When will we decide that enough is enough?!

Friends, it is confession time. Have you ever looked at someone's life and secretly thought, why can't I be her size, why can't I look like her, or why is her life better than mine? No, those do not ring a bell? What about how did she get a husband? She is pregnant and doesn't even like kids, or she doesn't even really go to church and she keeps getting blessed! Does any of that sound familiar? Ouch! I must admit, I have thought some of those thoughts before.

Before we know it, that jealousy causes us to begin comparing ourselves to everyone! It appears that everyone is living the life we want. We start to freak out thinking about what we do not have and what we feel we is missing. Next, we minimize our own lives and accomplishments. We wonder if anything we have is good enough. Then, the jealousy unfortunately leads us to rush and play catch up to make things happen. Sadly, we are only left feeling less than, frustrated, and inadequate.

Where is there room for contentment in all of that?

This jealousy issue really starts to manifest in high school if not sooner. I am sure you can remember young girls struggling to fit in and make lasting relationships. All of the pressure and awkwardness causes some girls to exhibit some jealous and nasty behaviors. It was such a difficult time for some. Girls constantly wanted to be like other girls, fought for the attention of boys, and competed for spots on athletic teams. It is no wonder that jealousy quickly reared its ugly head.

You may have even been the recipient of some of that cruel treatment. If things were that way when you and I were in school, can you even imagine what young girls face today? How do we prevent or protect them from these ungodly behaviors?

How is it that jealousy sneaks into our backpacks and follows us right into adulthood without us even noticing? The problem is that many of us never healed, from those past experiences, before leaving the hallways of high school. We eagerly leap out into the 'real-world' not even realizing that those seeds of jealousy have been planted deep down in our souls.

Well, what does jealousy do to our lives? There are some very nasty side effects of jealousy if we are not careful. One of the first things that springs up as a result of jealousy is bitterness. Bitterness has absolutely no manners. It will invade your soul and take over your heart. Bitterness will quickly harden your heart. We will talk more about that in the next chapter. James 3:14-15 (KJV) says it this way *but if ye have bitter envying and strife in your hearts, glory not, and lie not against the truth. This wisdom descendeth not from above, but is earthly, sensual, devilish.* In other words, bitter jealousy is not of God; it is of this world.

The next thing that happens in our lives as a consequence of jealousy is disorder. James 3:16 (KJV) goes on to say *for where envying and strife is, there is confusion and every evil work.* Jealousy always breeds disorder. The disorder may not always be on the outside. Sometimes the disorder is on the inside of us. One thing is for sure, disorder is not far behind when jealousy is present.

Think about the last time you witnessed a situation where one or both parties was dealing with jealousy. Would you say some disorder evolved from that situation? Let's go a little deeper. Think about the last time you felt jealous. Would you say that disorder quickly moved in whether through your actions or your mind?

I think you might agree that when jealousy is present a third thing always seems to happen. Our judgement is altered. It matters not what the reality of the situation is; we are only able to see it the way we want to see it. I have seen people become really jealous when someone else is honored in the workplace. They are not able to see that maybe the person deserved the honor because of his/her hard work. They are only able to see that they were overlooked.

The Bible takes it a step further and says *fret not thyself because of evildoers, neither be thou envious against the workers of iniquity* (Psalms 37:1 KJV). Why in the world would we be jealous of those who do wrong? Well, when our judgement is altered and we see something we want, that is all we can focus on. Suddenly, their lives look better than yours because they have what you desire. God warns us against this.

1 Corinthians 13:4 (KJV) *charity suffereth long, and is kind; charity envieth not; charity vaunteth not itself, is not puffed up.* Another version tells us that love is not jealous. Why is this important? Jealousy does not allow us to freely love others. The jealousy acts as a barrier and shuts off any love that would try and flow between the individuals. It is practically impossible to truly love someone when you want what they have or you struggle to even be happy for their successes. Even if you manage to work up a half smile or a "congratulations" the love is still hindered by the jealousy.

If the bitterness, disorder, altered judgement, and lack of love aren't convincing enough then maybe this last one will do it for you. Jealousy is like a cancer in your bones. You may be thinking that is a little extreme, but Proverbs 14:30 (KJV) says *a sound heart is the life of the flesh: but envy the rottenness of the bones.* Who knew that envy could have such an effect on the body? That just sounds horrible. It seems that God is trying to caution us that jealousy can and will affect our bodies, souls, and spirits.

So, what do we do? How can we rid our lives of jealousy? There are three things we can do that will really help free us from jealousy. The first is to celebrate with others! It seems like such an easy and obvious thing to do, but it can be difficult if we are struggling with a jealous spirit. We should be happy with and for others. When people share their good news, join in on the celebration! We are encouraged to rejoice with those that rejoice (Romans 12:15). Make a conscious effort to remove yourself from the situation entirely and participate in someone else's happiness. The truth is that we do not actually know what that person sacrificed to get what they have. We do not know how long they prayed or cried, but their time finally came and that deserves some rejoicing.

The second thing is that we must change our perspective. I know this is hard to internalize, but everything is not about you and I. Sometimes, we are just not a factor in the situation. If our perspective is that it is always about us, then jealousy will always have a chance in our lives. We have to acknowledge that it may be his turn or her turn right now. That is alright. You have to trust that when the timing is right, then it will be about you, so there is no reason to be jealous.

The third and final thing you have to do if you are going to take control of jealousy is concentrate on you. That means you have to worry more about what God is doing in your life and less about what is happening in the lives of others. You have to be confident and know who God called you to be! You have to trust that everything He has for you will manifest in your life at the appropriate time.

When you are concentrating on you, your focus is on God because you do not want to miss what He is doing. You can confidently compose yourself in contentment because you know that your God will come through. Besides, Psalm 84:11 (KJV) says ...*the Lord will give grace and glory: no good thing will he withhold from them that walk uprightly*. Ask yourself a question: Am I doing what is right before the Lord? If your answer is yes, then just believe that He will not withhold any good thing from you!

As I reflect on this tough lesson, I think about a little second grade girl I taught some years ago. It was an exciting day in our classroom. It was one of those times that all students look forward to. We were quickly approaching a holiday, so we were having our classroom holiday party. If you know anything about school-aged children, then you know that nothing brings excited and anticipation like a classroom party!

All of the students had their plates with chips and their juice boxes on the desks. I started in the front of the classroom and was making my way around delivering the cupcakes. That little girl sat way in the back of the room. As I passed out the cupcakes on the front row, one of the little boys turned around to the students in the back and waved his cupcake in the air to show them that he had one and they did not. Then, he turned it up a notch and in a very taunting manner, like only a second grade boy can do, he asked, "are you all jealous?!" Now, before I could even give him my ever-so-scary teacher look (that warned you better cut it out) the little girl in the back of the room spoke up and said, "Now why would we be jealous when our cupcake is on the way?" Wow! Such wisdom in the second grade!

If only we could see things from that little girl's perspective! When we see God handing out blessings to others or people moving ahead in life are we capable of seeing that there is no need to be jealous because ours is on the way? Are you content enough to sit calmly in the back as God makes His way around?

<h2 style="text-align:center">▶ | ◀ Personal Reflection ▶ | ◀</h2>

1.   *What is it that causes jealousy to stir inside of you?*

2.   *Specifically, how is jealousy standing in the way of your contentment?*

3.   *What is one thing you can implement quickly to push jealousy out of your life?*

Don't let jealousy hold you back; release it and confidently walk into your future. Begin by praying this prayer:

Heavenly Father,

I thank you for all that you have planned for my life. I realize that I do not have to be jealous for what anyone else has. Please forgive me for the times when I let jealousy damage me. Teach me to be confident with my life and the timeline that it is on. Help me to be content because I know that you will not withhold any good thing from me.   In Jesus' Name I pray, Amen.

Contentment is believing God even when you struggle to believe.

Chapter Six

Healing for the Hardened Heart

When you hear the word 'heart' what immediately comes to mind? You may think about a little, red shape or if you are like most women, you probably begin thinking about love, emotions, and/or other sweet, mushy, gushy things. However, the heart is much deeper than that. The heart is very complex. What exactly is the function of the heart? What does it take to have a healthy heart? The heart is the key organ in the circulatory system. As a hollow, muscular pump, its main function is to propel blood throughout the body.

In the process of sending blood through the body, many conditions and diseases can occur which can keep the heart from functioning properly. As a society, we talk a lot about having a healthy heart (in the natural physical realm), but do we give the same attention to having a healthy heart as it relates to the spiritual? While a hardened heart is not an actual medical condition of the heart, it is most certainly a spiritual condition.

This spiritual heart condition hinders the blood (Blood of Jesus) from flowing properly through the body (body of Christ) by way of a person's life. We will explore that further a little later.

What does a woman with a hardened heart really look like? Well, to the natural eye, she does not look different from any other woman. She is well groomed, smiles often, and makes small talk with all those she meets. She works a regular job, maybe owns her own business, but she is successful at whatever she does. She has a small circle of close loved ones. She attends church regularly. She gives back to her community. She probably interacts normally on social media. She looks just like you and I. She is an everyday woman. How would we recognize her?

It is only through careful examination of her words and actions that the true condition of her heart is actually revealed.

Matthew 15:18 (KJV) says it this way *but those things which proceed out of the mouth come forth from the heart; and they defile the man.* The woman whose heart has become hardened may say things like, "I do not really trust anybody", "people always let me down", or "I do not know if God is going to come through in this situation". Her actions may be very guarded towards people; she may only let people see/know so much about her life. She may refuse to begin new relationships/friendships. Maybe she attends church, but shuns away from really getting involved.

Sometimes we become skeptical of everyone. We lash out at people and end up missing out on godly connections; as a result we only end up with surface-level relationships…if that. As our hearts harden, we see people experiencing loving and lasting relationships while we seem to only experience betrayal. Friends, make no mistake about it, women are not the only ones affected by this spiritual heart condition. While the woman is used as a reference here, the same 'condition' can apply to men as well.

A hardened heart not only affects the woman, but it affects those connected to her, and all those she comes in contact with. She may never speak it aloud, but in the deep crevices of her heart she feels rejected, broken, guarded and maybe even isolated. She was not born this way; she did not intend to live her life this way. Life just happened…

Do you know this woman? Can you relate? Perhaps, this woman is you.

Have you ever felt like you were not good enough which left you feeling hurt and betrayed? Oftentimes, someone or some specific situation leaves us with those nasty feelings. You may be thinking I will **never** get hurt like this again. Why would God let me get hurt like this in the first place? Those thoughts we discussed in chapter one, begin to swirl through your mind.

Everyone is against me. No one can be trusted; I do not need anyone.

Before we know it, we have built a little barb-wire fence around our hearts to keep everyone out. The result is that we begin pushing everyone away as our hearts turn harder and harder towards people…and God. You feel like no one ever shows you mercy, so you refuse to show mercy to anyone else. Your heart may scream that the person did not deserve to be shown mercy. How about if your heart was broken. We all know that is a horrible feeling. Did you make a vow to yourself that you would never forgive the person who broke your heart? Your heart may be tightening at this very moment just thinking about it. Maybe you can feel yourself beginning to get angry.

You can probably even remember every last detail of the incident. God wants to challenge us to identify the underlying causes of anger and the steps we should take to control it. What we do not see is how anger affects our hearts. It is unavoidable, people and circumstances will make us angry from time to time.

Even Jesus got angry, but He sinned not. We must strive to be like Him, deal with our anger, and keep an open heart. How we respond to the anger is important. Anger and contentment simply cannot coexist. How do we remain calm and control our anger in stressful situations?

Ephesians 4:26 (KJV) states *be ye angry, and sin not: let not the sun go down upon your wrath:* You may feel anger about an injustice or some ungodly behavior that has happened to you, but how do you react to that? We are instructed to sin not. Someone else's sin does not give us the right to go and sin as well. You may feel like cussing, going out and being reckless with your body, or getting revenge, but then you sinned too.

The sins we commit push us further away from God only to be left with our little hardened hearts full of hurt. The other part of the scripture says not to let the sun go down on our anger. In other words, we need to get over it pretty quickly. Essentially, we have less than 24 hours to be angry, release the anger, and move on. That is not to say that the pain or damage will go away as quickly, but the anger must go.

Why should I let go of my anger?

Well, because anger festers. Anger is like a pot of boiling water on a stove. The longer it sits there the hotter it gets. Then, it begins to rise to the surface until it boils over. The sooner the release takes place then the sooner we are able to receive the healing that we need to move on.

Hold your head up, sister, you are not a bad person. Your desire is to love freely, have fruitful relationships, have a mended heart, and be able to be transparent just like everyone else. How do we get there from here? Can this 'heart condition' be reversed? The answer is indeed yes!

The problem is that a hardened heart will never allow you or I to live the content life that God has designed for us. We will never be able to truly thrive if we continue that way. The fact is that contentment cannot and will not be contained inside of a heart that has been hardened. It just is not possible because the fruits of the spirit cannot develop in those conditions.

Why does it matter? Well, this is critical because the development of the fruits of the spirit (love, joy, peace, patience, kindness, goodness, faithfulness, gentleness, and self-control) directly correlates with having a free heart and living a life full of contentment.

It is God's desire that these fruits are perfected in our lives. What kind of life are we living if we do not have and exhibit love, joy and peace? Have you ever met a believer lacking one of these fruits? They were not that pleasant were they? How can we claim to be Jesus' representative in the earth when we lack patience and do not treat people with kindness and goodness? The life of a Christian is an ongoing journey and lack of faithfulness, gentleness or self-control make it difficult to be an effective witness. As you can see, hearts that are hardened will shut out all that God is trying to grow inside of us.

I was happily driving home from work one Friday afternoon, when all of a sudden, I had to slow down to a complete stop as traffic was backed up all the way down the highway. I strained to try and see up ahead. I thought maybe I could see what was going on. *What in the world was the hold up?* After inching along for about 45 minutes, I finally made it close enough to see. There had been an accident which caused a roadblock. The barrier (roadblock) would not allow us to continue; the flow of traffic had been hindered.

It was then that I considered this must be what it is like when we have hardened hearts. God's love tries to get through, but the flow of the Holy Spirit is hindered due to our heart condition. Have you ever seen a dam created in a river or stream? This too, (a barrier created that obstructs the flow of water) is an illustration of the hindrance our hard hearts can cause.

The good news is that God wants us to recover and it is never too late for a spiritual heart surgery. After people experience heart disease or other heart conditions, doctors advise that immediate lifestyle changes must be made. There are some things that cannot be continued and other things that must be implemented immediately. The wise advice of doctors can be applied to spiritual heart conditions as well. If we are going to recover, then a lifestyle change is required.

Through much prayer and the 5 R's, recovery is possible! The 5 R's are repent, release, read, retrain, and receive. The key is that each of these has to be properly applied through prayer. If we are going to soften the ground of our hardened hearts then the first 'R', which is to repent is a top priority. We must first acknowledge that our hearts have hardened towards God and people. That can be very difficult to admit, but freedom comes when we are honest about it. Next, we should pray asking Him to forgive us and then believe that we are forgiven. Then, we trust that there is no condemnation in Christ so we are free from guilt. We can move forward. Once we turn from our wicked ways, all is forgotten. The moment we repent, our hearts begin to soften.

I know what you are thinking, "why should I repent when I was the one that was done wrong." That may be true, but when you search deep down inside you will see that you have been angry with that person or God and that requires repentance. You may have let that frustration turn into bitterness and God does not want you to live like that. Jeremiah 17:9 KJV cautions us *the heart is deceitful above all things, and desperately wicked: who can know it?* This is why it is so important to embed each of these R's in prayer. As you pray, the Holy Spirit will tell you specifically why you need to repent. It may be something that you did not even consider.

As you are prayerfully seeking God with a repentant heart, the second 'R', release, must be addressed. What are you releasing? Well, you may be releasing a person, a situation, or a particular event. You may need to release a situation that did not work out the way you planned or something painful that happened to you. You may need to release a person that you have been angry with for hurting you. Matthew 6:15 (KJV) states *but if ye forgive not men their trespasses, neither will your Father forgive your trespasses.* This scripture is trying to get us to understand that if we do not forgive others, God will not forgive us. You have to release them because whatever happened is not worth you not being forgiven. I know, I can see the tears running down your face, and I can hear your soul crying out.

I just cannot let it go. I will not forgive them.

As your sister in Christ, understand that I say this in love; you have got to release it. You must release it if you are ever going to be the person God created you to be. If you are ever going to live a life of contentment, then it must be released. Again, this is why you must carefully walk through each of the R's in prayer. It is just too difficult to do on your own. Be honest with God; tell Him that you are having a hard time releasing. He will help you. He already knows anyway; you might as well be honest with Him. He knows that your father abandoned you, He knows that your boyfriend betrayed you, and He knows that your mother gave you away. He knows that your siblings dislike you, He knows that your co-workers turned on you, and He even knows your friend lied on you. He knows. Ask Him to help you release it and as He does, you will feel a release in your heart as well.

When recovering from a hardened heart the third 'R' is read. We must read the Word of God daily. The Word of God is living and still has power. If you do not know where to begin, try starting with Psalm 51:10 (KJV) *create in me a clean heart, O God: and renew a right spirit within me.* Just read it over and over until it begins to sink in. As you read, pray and ask God to lead you to other scriptures that will help heal your heart. Even if He just reveals one or two scriptures to you that is a great place to start. You will quickly find that the Word will be like medicine to your heart and soul.

The Word of God will work like a jackhammer on the ground of your heart.

The next 'R' is to retrain. If we are truly going to recover, then we have to retrain our minds to think about people differently. In spite of our past difficulties, we must look for the good in people. If we are going to have fruitful relationships then we must let people into our hearts and lives. Of course, this is done cautiously and over time. Prayerfully ask the Holy Spirit to retrain your mind and show you the people you can get close to. Pray about the people that you enter in relationships, friendships, and partnerships with. It is unfair for you to miss out on the vital connections that we all need with people. It is also unfair to make people pay for the past mistakes of others. As you retrain your mind your perception of others will change and your heart will be open to receive.

The final 'R' is receive. As you prayerfully repent, release, read, and retrain you will become ready to receive all that God has in store for you. God wants you to receive a heart like His. He wants to walk you through this recovery process so that your heart will be a reflection of His. Our Father wants you to receive a heart overflowing with love. You will receive a content heart that the Holy Spirit can flow through unhindered.

At the beginning of this chapter, we discussed that a spiritual heart condition hinders the blood (Blood of Jesus) from flowing properly through the body (body of Christ) by way of a person's life. Just like a heart condition hinders blood from flowing through your physical heart. There is so much power in the Blood of Jesus! By accessing that power and allowing the Holy Spirit to flow freely we are able to be used mightily by God. It is His desire to use you tremendously for the Kingdom. When the Blood is flowing freely through your heart, then you are able to extend your reach and affect the Body of Christ in a positive way. Are you ready for your heart reversal?

▶ | ◀ Personal Reflection ▶ | ◀

1. *Would you say that people's actions and/or difficult situations have caused your heart to harden?*

2. *Could contentment be a possibility for you if your heart was healed?*

3. *Which of the 5 R's do you find to be the most difficult?*

If you are going to walk in contentment, recovery from a hardened heart is a requirement. Begin by praying this prayer:

Heavenly Father,

I thank you for caring about the condition of my heart. Sometimes it is hard for me to recognize that my heart has become hardened. I repent now for turning my heart against you and others. I release every person that has hurt me and every situation that I have still been holding on to. Please direct me as I read your Word daily. Let your Word be healing to me. Retrain me to think about things and people in a different way. Help me to recover so that I can receive everything that you have for me. I thank you in advance that my heart is turning back to you. In Jesus' Name I pray, Amen.

Chapter Seven

Press Pause

Do you know what drives me crazy? Waiting. I feel like we are always waiting on one thing or another. If you are like me, then at some point in time, you have probably thought *I do not have time to wait.* From the minor, waiting in the line at the grocery store to the major, waiting on God for a prayer request, it can all be quite nerve-wrecking.   Then, it is the little things that almost send me over the edge. For instance, why is the wait so long in the 10 items or less line at the store? Why do they always ask you to pull up and wait some more in the drive-thru line once you have already made it to the window? I just do not understand these things. Sometimes it just seems like a conspiracy, but I believe our Heavenly Father is trying to perfect patience in me. I do not know if I am passing the tests. Please keep me lifted in prayer.

The fact of the matter is that I have gotten a whole lot better with this process called waiting, but it can still be a real struggle at times. Oftentimes, we just feel like time is running out. One cannot help but wonder how long the wait is going to last. In this chapter, we will consider the thought that impatience breeds discontentment in our lives. I know we do not want to discuss patience because it is really hard to wait. Trust me, I know. When there are things we desire, we want those things to come to pass quickly. When they tarry, we become very impatient. Then, we secretly begin to wonder if God is really going to come through.

It is especially difficult to wait when we feel that we have waited long enough or that God has revealed certain things to us that shall be. *Lord, if you said it would happen, what in the world am I still waiting on?* We silently wonder what the holdup is if God promised not to withhold any good thing from our lives. Although we may feel like impatiently skipping past this chapter it is imperative that we press pause and examine this topic. Together, we will learn how to slow down, gather ourselves, and patiently wait on God.

I think the first thing we have to accept is that waiting is just a part of life. We all have waited and we all will wait again. No amount of money or even status can eliminate waiting from life. So, if waiting is inevitable then the question is not how do we avoid waiting, but rather how do we become good at waiting. How do we wait in a way that pleases God? God never leaves us stranded to figure these things out on our own. He gives us a strategy in Psalms 37:7 (KJV) *rest in the Lord, and wait patiently for him: fret not thyself because of him who prospereth in his way, because of the man who bringeth wicked devices to pass.*

Well, we say things like wait on God, be patient, and rest in the Lord all the time, but what does that really look like? How do we make that practical and apply it to our everyday lives? If we are ever going to effectively apply this verse of scripture to our lives then there are just a few things we must do.

If we are going to rest in the Lord and wait patiently on Him, then the first thing we must do is sense what God is doing. God cannot and will not be rushed. Take a moment and let that settle into your spirit. We simply cannot force God to adhere to our timelines. It would sure make you and I feel better, but our God does not work that way. The choice is ours, we can continually wrestle with God and try to get Him to move at the pace we like (losing the battle every time) or we can rest in Him and move at His pace. Believe me, I have tried everything to get God to speed things up in my life and we keep ending with the same result. I get all tired and worn out while God just keeps on watching and waiting for me to rest in Him. It is exhausting! I finally had to say, "Lord, you win…I'll just wait on you because this is too much"! I can imagine our loving Father as He smiles, leans over to His right and says to Jesus, "Finally, she gets it"!

Friend, the choice is yours, too. Will you keep fighting it or just choose to wait on Him? The cold, hard reality is that we have to sense what God is doing because some seasons are about development and preparation which can include a lot of waiting. If we sense that God is developing us, then we will not be in such a hurry to move on. We will realize that He is preparing us to be successful in the next season. God is more concerned with developing our character than He is with moving us swiftly through various seasons.

Now, I am not suggesting that you will be happy about the wait at first. However, it will work to your advantage if you are cooperative. Over time, you will be able to sense what God is teaching you and where He wants you to concentrate your prayers and efforts. It may not be in the area you were originally thinking. For example, you may be waiting to launch your own business and you think that you are just waiting on the financial resources, but suppose God wants to work compassion in you before you interact with your future customers? You could be waiting on God for a spouse and you think that you are waiting for God to send the right person. Suppose God needs to develop grace and forgiveness in you first? We have to keep in mind that we only have a limited perspective while God sees the whole picture.

The same is true when God is preparing to make a move in our lives. We have to be able to sense it and cooperate. There may be things you need to do, take a Bible class, brush up on your writing skills, get additional vocal training etc. Whatever it is, if we become frustrated in the wait and begin to drag our feet we are then hindering the process.

In my last waiting season, I was petitioning God for a particular prayer request. God kept telling me that He had that situation under control but I needed to work on my writing more. I could not understand what writing had to do with my particular prayer request, so I wrote here and there and dragged my feet a little. Did you know that delayed obedience was disobedience? God revealed to me that it all worked together, I just could not see the connection. His continual response to me was to write! Needless to say, I got to writing! Had I been more patient and quietly resting in Him then I would have been able to sense what He was doing. When we are able to sense what He is doing then we are able to rest because we understand that we need whatever He is doing/teaching for our development.

The second thing we must do if we are going to rest and wait patiently on the Lord is set our minds on what God is doing. Chances are your life does not look the way you want it to right now. You may know that God has amazing things in store for you, but nothing around you is suggesting that. *Set your affection on things above, not on things on the earth* (Colossians 3:2, KJV). You have to keep your mind so focused on what God said and what He is doing in your life that nothing will change your mind. When you are able to do this then you can rest and wait because you know whatever He said will surely happen.

It does not matter what season of life you are in, what other people have to say about or even what doctors have to say about it. If God said it, then it should be settled in your mind. You may be a seasoned woman, but if God said you will have a baby, start a business, or launch out into ministry then I dare you to just set your mind on what He said! You are then able to press pause and rest right in Him.

Thirdly, you have to shut out the distractions. Won't people just let the enemy use them when you are trying to wait patiently on God?

"You're not married yet, when do you plan on finding a man?"

"You've been married for a while now, when are you having some babies?"

"I thought you would have started that business when you were much younger…"

"With your financial situation how are you going to own your own home?"

"Are you still in college? I thought you would have graduated by now."

Has anyone ever made any of these comments to you? They sure can sting a little bit, can't they?   People have no idea that their invasive questions/comments could be the very thing that you are taking to God in prayer daily.

They have no idea how a light-hearted comment to them could be the very thing that causes your heart to weep.

While some people are deliberately trying to be unkind, others can just be somewhat insensitive. Lord, help us to be sensitive to others. I wish we would take the time to think how our comments may affect others. I wish we would be more sensitive to the Holy Spirit when we speak with one another. I wish we would let Him speak through us to offer words of healing instead of words of hurt.

The important thing to remember is that we cannot control what others say or do. We can only shut out the distractions as they occur. We have to be so comfortable resting in the Father, as we wait on Him, that we do not even flinch when these distractions come our way.

Resting in the Lord and waiting patiently for Him gives us time to do the fourth thing which is to sanctify ourselves. No point in just sitting around idly! Resting and waiting on the Lord is different from resting and waiting as in relaxation. There must be some action involved! You cannot just sit and twiddle your thumbs because you do not know how long your season of waiting will last. Once it ends, you do not want to look back and see that you wasted time. You have to make the most of it. As you sanctify yourself, you will begin to pray and study the Word like never before. The more time you spend in prayer, the more He will show you things that must go. There are things that must be cut away before you can move forward.

Your goal should be to cultivate a deeper relationship with Christ.

The more you put into your sanctification process, the better you will be on the other side. God will teach you as He sanctifies you. He will teach you about prayer, praise and true worship. He will teach you to abide in Him. He will work with you like clay until you look more like Him. This process is often referred to as pruning. He cuts away all that must go and puts on all that you need for the next season.

Sanctification is a very private and painful process.

Wait patiently on Him as He sanctifies you. Just know that anything you put above God or desire more than Him will be cut away. All of your fleshly thoughts and desires will be cut away. Anything that does not align with the Will of God will be cut away. Anyone who is keeping you from your destiny will be cut away. You know that thing or person that is not good for you, but you just cannot seem to let go of it? Don't you worry and don't you be surprised because God will cut it away as He sanctifies you.

If our lives are like a little seed plant, then patience is the fertilizer that develops the seed into a beautiful garden of contentment. Developing patience causes us to rest and be satisfied with where we are.

► | ◄ Personal Reflection ► | ◄

1. *Do you find waiting to be difficult?*

2. *When was the last time you were able to completely rest in the Lord and wait on Him?*

3. *What is it that keeps you from resting in the Lord? What will you do to work on that?*

If you are ready to press pause and start cultivating contentment, begin by praying this prayer:

Heavenly Father,

I thank you that I have the option to rest in you. I do not always find it easy to do that. Please forgive me for the times when I have moved ahead of you. Oftentimes, I struggle to wait patiently on you. I feel anxious when things do not happen as quickly as I would like for them to. Slow me down. Teach me what it truly means to rest in you. Teach me to truly wait on you. Develop patience in me that I may be able to live contently in any season. In Jesus' Name I pray, Amen.

Chapter Eight

Peace not Pieces

Why is my life such a mess?

I did not sign up for this?

I just do not have enough hours in the day!

Does any of that sound familiar to you? How many women do you know that share these same feelings? Time and time again, our busy everyday lives rob us of our peace and leave us feeling panicked and anxious. While we would all like to live peaceful and productive lives, we end up feeling crushed and in pieces. How does this continue to happen to us? What are we doing wrong?

I just cannot do this anymore…

Many times a day this thought races through our minds. What woman wants the world to know that her fragile life has slipped out of her hands like a piece of dinnerware and shattered on the hard kitchen floor?

Well, of course none of us want the world to know that! It becomes obvious to us that our lives are spiraling out of control. Yet, that is to be expected as we frantically multi-task, run here and there, meet deadlines, return phone calls, clean our houses, and search through emails all while being everything to everyone! We feel like we are always trying to 'catch up'. When we actually do get caught up, new tasks appear before we even have time to take a deep breath. Wow, I feel anxious just thinking about it! Why does it seem like everyone else is living a well-planned out, perfectly productive life?

Living a life in pieces threatens to steal the victorious life that God intends for each of us to live.

I can remember one season of my life where I was operating in everything but peace. At that particular time, I was running around here, there, and everywhere. I was living in city A, working in city B, and going to class in city C. Needless to say, I had quite a commute most days. I had many sleepy mornings and long days that followed. I would wake up early commute to city B and then work all day. On Tuesdays and Thursdays, immediately following work, I would commute to class in city C for several more hours. As if that were not enough, on some of those days I would leave class, head back to city A and end the evening with a meeting or service at church. I cannot even tell you how tired I would be at night.

My mind would be swirling with all of the information. I had a lot of responsibilities at work that included meetings, planning activities, and assisting my principal at a minimum. In class, I had to participate in discussions, submit assignments, and complete internship hours. There was plenty to do at church as well because we have a very active church; there was always work to be done.

It was just a blessing that I did not turn in my homework at church and schedule a prayer meeting with my professor! Everything was running all together! I was wearing myself out. I had no peace and an empty tank! Why do we do that to ourselves? Well, because we have goals to accomplish and tasks to check off of our ever-so-important to-do lists. But, at what cost? Is it really worth it? My vote would be no.

Although we could all use a little more peace, the reality is that we cannot pack it up, head to a secluded island and get the much needed peace and rest that we deserve. We also cannot hide away from life and refuse to be bothered. The key is to manage our time and become efficient at multi-tasking. The other rather obvious bit of truth is that we cannot escape pain and problems either. That is why contentment is so important.

Contentment comes when there is peace in the presence of pain and problems.

Philippians 4:6-7 (KJV) says *be careful for nothing; but in every thing by prayer and supplication with thanksgiving let your requests be made known unto God. And the peace of God, which passeth all understanding, shall keep your hearts and minds through Christ Jesus.* If we are ever going to have peace in the midst of being consumed and overworked then we must use this passage of scripture as a guide.

Be careful for nothing can also be translated as be anxious for nothing. It is really hard not to be anxious. Especially when it comes to things that are important to us. We spend a lot of time dealing with anxiety but Matthew 6:27 (KJV) asks *which of you by taking thought can add one cubit unto his stature?* Simply put, can we even add an hour to our lives by being anxious? The answer is no, we cannot.

I believe some of the anxiety comes from us putting too much pressure on ourselves to be perfect. We want our neighbors, friends, and co-workers to all think that we are living these perfectly managed lives. But why? We know that none of our lives are perfect, so we must stop getting ourselves all worked up. Our anxiety quickly erupts into panic and before we know it, we are drowning in a pool of panic. The problem is that panic proposes that God is not present in our predicament. We know that is not true. God is always present in our troubles. We have to choose to stop when we feel the anxiousness and pray immediately.

Although our lives are busy, we have to deliberately make time to pray. You may be thinking that your day-to-day schedule is already maxed out, but you will find that peace will begin to enter into your body as you spend time with God. You need peace, right? Well, then you must make sacrifices. You may start by giving Him a few minutes in the morning, in the car, or on your lunch break. When you put forth the effort to look, you will find the time. You would be surprised what a few minutes in His presence will do for you. He will give you more energy to maximize the day. He may give you fresh eyes to see your schedule in a different way; revealing to you ways to gain some time back. He may send you help to lighten your load. One thing is for sure, you will never know until you make time and try.

Just take it one day at a time. Sometimes we get overwhelmed trying to plan out our entire week. On Monday, we find ourselves stressed about things we have to do on Thursday. We feel the panic try to creep in, but Matthew 6:34 (KJV) instructs *take therefore no thought for the morrow: for the morrow shall take thought for the things of itself. Sufficient unto the day is the evil thereof.* Taking it one day at a time will lift some of the burden.

The Word says through prayer and petition which means to share your requests with Him. In the beginning it may be as simple as "Lord, help me to better schedule my day and give me your peace as I do it." He will honor you for taking the time to meet with Him. That may not be a one-time prayer, you may have to pray it daily. That is petition.

Not only are we told to make our requests known to God through prayer, but we are to do it with thanksgiving. I know you feel overwhelmed because you are working two jobs, and raising a family, but you still have something to be thankful for. I know your leadership role has you stretched too thin and people pull on you all day, but you still have something to be thankful for. Begin by thanking Him for the job and/or family He has given you. Keep in mind that there are people who are constantly looking for a job and several others who would love to have a family.

When you take the time to think about it, there are so many things to actually be grateful for. As you begin to think about all that He has done for you, thankfulness will move peace right into your heart and move anxiousness right out.

Martha, the sister of Mary and Lazarus, found herself dealing with this same issue. She too, struggled to maintain her peace. *And Jesus answered and said unto her, Martha, Martha, thou art careful and troubled about many things:* (Luke 10:41 KJV) Why did Jesus say that to her? The story is found in Luke chapter 10 verses 38-42. Well, Martha must have heard that Jesus and His disciples were passing through town, so she invited Him into her home.

Imagine the panic she must have felt! Having Jesus over for dinner?! Think about all of the cleaning that would require. I mean, you cannot invite JESUS over to your dusty house with dirty dishes in the sink. Where would He sit? On top of the clean laundry thrown on the couch waiting to be folded? Well, of course not. What was He going to eat? You do not serve our Savior some sandwich you threw together on old bread! Can't you just see poor Martha working herself into a panic attack? Don't you laugh; you know you and I would be the same way.

I am sure that Martha did not want Jesus and the disciples to think that her life was in pieces. She goes over to Jesus and asks Him to tell her sister to help her and that is when He told her she was worried about too many things. I am sure that is not the response she was expecting. Quiet your soul and look back at verse 41; this time insert your name. Is that what Jesus is saying to you right now?

If we are modern-day Marthas then we must make the choice for peace.

Earlier in this chapter, I shared that contentment comes when there is peace in the presence of pain and problems. There will always be problems in life and there will be seasons of pain as well. It is during those times that we must cling to God more tightly than ever before. As we cling to Him, His peace will change us. Even if the pain does not go right away or the problem is not solved immediately, His peace will allow you to remain content until the change occurs.

When I think of peace and what that looks like, I automatically think of my great grandmother Mamie Cooper. She was just the epitome of grace and peace. She was 94 years old when she left this earth, but I do not remember ever seeing her in pieces. She was always full of peace. Peaceful in the mornings, peaceful in the evenings, just peaceful all day long!

As children, my cousins and I would stay with her and my aunt after-school and all-day during the summers. Mamie would have a smile on her face all day long. Whether she was sitting in her chair watching TV or cooking in the kitchen, peace was her constant companion. We all know that having several young children running around the house all day can quickly shift your peace, but that was not the case for Mamie. She would pray, sing, and read her Bible all day. As a child, I can remember constantly wondering, how anyone could pray that much! Was there even that much to say? As I have gotten older, I have discovered that there certainly is that much to pray about all day long. My mother remembers Mamie the same way and she knew her longer than I did. No matter what happened in life or with the family she just refused to let anything or anyone steal her peace. As a result of her life, I know that it is possible to live a life full of peace. We just have to be determined to make it happen in our own lives.

▶ | ◀ **Personal Reflection** ▶ | ◀

1. *What is it that continually tries to steal your peace?*

2. *When you experienced peace in the past, what caused that to happen?*

3. *What is one practical thing you can do today to have peace?*

If you are going to experience peacefully content days then begin by praying this prayer:

Heavenly Father,

I thank you that peace is available to me. There are many days when I feel like my life is in pieces. Help me to put those pieces back together so I can experience a full life. When anxiety and panic try to steal my peace, please help me to turn to you immediately. Teach me to be anxious for nothing. Give me a thankful heart and help me to make my requests known to you. I give all of my troubles, to-do lists, and tasks to you. In Jesus' Name I pray, Amen.

Chapter Nine

Saying 'Yes' to Surrender

Who knew living for Jesus meant giving up your life and laying it *all* down? That is what true surrender entails. What does it take to live a truly surrendered life unto Christ? It surely is not always easy or comfortable. Women who say 'yes' to surrender simultaneously turn their backs on selfishness. Surrender requires less and less of oneself and more and more of Jesus. It may sound simple, but try telling your flesh that it is no longer in control. Inform your flesh that Jesus is the new boss of your life and see if there is not a struggle. There must be ways to minimize our selfish nature and keep that 'terrible toddler mentality' suppressed. When we focus on putting God's plan for our lives first, self-succumbs to surrender and contentment naturally follows.

If you have been in church for any length of time, then I am sure at some point or another you stood proudly singing out the lyrics to *I Surrender All*. *All to Jesus I surrender; all to Him I freely give.* We have all sang those lyrics, right? We sing it so loud and proud. Yet, have we really processed what we are saying? Think carefully before you answer. We are professing that everything in our lives, everything that is important to us, we lay it all at the feet of Jesus. Everything. Sometimes, I think we believe that we truly have done that. Until, God holds up our plans or asks for more of us. Gulp. We start thinking about all of the things we want. We want what we want when we want it. We start believing that God has forgotten us because He is not answering our prayers. Instantly, we begin feeling frustrated and impatient. Where is the surrender in all of that?

If we would be honest with ourselves, the truth of the matter is that we have no problem surrendering to God until He interferes with our will.   Now, that is where we draw the line. *Lord, I will surrender to you, but just let me live my life the way I want to.* Friends, I have an announcement to make and it may just mess you up. Brace yourself. God is not concerned with your will or your plan. If you truly surrender to Him, you will not be living the life *you* want to live; you will be living the life **He** wants you to live. Whew, that was tough, but we got through it. God is waiting for each of us to truly surrender and align ourselves with His Will.

It happens to the best of us, doesn't it? We look around and see that our will (the things we want) is just not happening. So, we begin to pray ineffective prayers. Oh yes, prayers can be ineffective. Prayers that do not align with the Will of God are pointless and ineffective. Then, we end up wrestling with God; trying to convince Him to do what we want Him to do. That is one battle we will never win, so it is just exhausting!

You know, one of my favorite scriptures perfectly illustrates this thought. Psalm 37:4 (KJV) says *delight thyself also in the Lord: and he shall give thee the desires of thine heart.* My whole life, I thought, oh this is great, if I just delight in God, then He will give me what I want. That sounds great, right? Well, a couple of years ago, God gave me a fresh revelation pertaining to that scripture. What the scripture is *really* saying is that when I delight in God, then He will give me what to want. In other words, He will lead me and say this is what I want you to desire or that is not what I want you to desire. Well, that changes everything! This scripture is really talking about surrender. Surrendering the things you and I want for the things He wants us to want.

Have you ever seen a toddler in the grocery store who was denied a toy or some candy? Man, some of those little people just completely lose it! This one little boy cleared the aisle, knocked things off the shelves, and then stretched completely out in the floor! While his poor, humiliated mother tried to quickly and quietly get him up off the floor. All because he did not get what he wanted. We shake our heads in disbelief when we see these scenes taking place, but how often do we do this with God? Have you ever thrown a 'tantrum' and lost all control when God did not give you what you wanted? Now, you probably did not tear up the grocery store because we, as adults, are much more subtle with our tantrums. Perhaps, you decided to give God the silent treatment, not go to church and not read your Bible. Maybe you decided you would just go out and make things happen on your own. God wants His children to be free from tantrums and surrendered to Him.

Surrender is so very important as it relates to contentment. There is just a natural correlation between the two. When we lay it all before Jesus entirely then we can be content with whatever situation we are facing because we know that we are in the Will of God. Contentment will just become your character because you know that God will not allow anything to hinder His Will.

Why is it so hard to surrender? There are so many scriptures on this topic. The theme seems to be consistent: we must die to self. That means once we are in Christ, we have to die to our old ways. We have to know that we were crucified with Christ; our flesh, passions, and desires must die. Galatians 2:20 (KJV) says *I am crucified with Christ: nevertheless I live; yet not I, but Christ liveth in me: and the life which I now live in the flesh I live by the faith of the Son of God, who loved me, and gave himself for me.* Sometimes, we like to say things like, "Yeah, I love Jesus, but I'm human; I still like to drink, cuss, party, smoke, etc." You just feel free to insert whatever it is that you struggle to give up.

The Bible tells us that we have to be dead to sin, that we have to deny ourselves, and we must put off the old self. If we are going to live a truly surrendered life then we have to be made new in Christ. Ephesians 4:22-24 (KJV) says it this way *that ye put off concerning the former conversation the old man, which is corrupt according to the deceitful lusts; And be renewed in the spirit of your mind; And that ye put on the new man, which after God is created in righteousness and true holiness.* It is so hard to truly surrender because ultimately, we are no longer slaves to sin which causes us to suffer in our bodies. We also realize that we have to become less (John 3:30).

I cannot speak for anyone else; I can only speak for myself. Surrender is not easy. It is a constant battle with the flesh as we make it submit to the Will of God. It is difficult to do, but we must win the battle. Whenever there is something that we desire, we must surrender it to the Will of God. If it is God's Will then He will make it happen. If it is not His Will then we must allow the desire to die.

As difficult as it is, I believe it is definitely possible. We must strive to live a totally surrendered life to Christ. So, what does that look like? Someone who is totally surrendered to God is set free from sin, Christ lives in them and they have taken up their cross to follow Him. This person is set free and Jesus is center stage! *And he said to them all, If any man will come after me, let him deny himself, and take up his cross daily, and follow me.* (Luke 9:23 KJV)

When you and I fully surrender to God, we become alive to God in Christ, we put on a new self, and recognize that He must become greater in our lives. When Christ becomes greater, He matter much more than anything we desire. He becomes our sole focus and His Will becomes our will. As we die to self, in a beautiful turn of events, we become more like Him and we just yearn to live for the Will of God.

Often, when people are in the presence of God they lift their hands to Him. Lifting your hands to God is a sign of worship, but it is also a sign of surrender. When you lift your hands to God you are saying that you are ready to lay down your will, desire, need, or whatever else before Him. When we lift both hands to Him, it is practically impossible to physically hold onto to anything in that position. Try it; try to hold onto any object while you have both hands lifted in the air. You see, the same is true spiritually. We cannot hold onto things when we are truly surrendered to Him. Contentment will come when you release it all and lift your hands to Him in surrender.

▶ | ◀ Personal Reflection ▶ | ◀

1.   *What is it that keeps you from surrendering to God?*

2.   *Do you truly trust that God's Will is better for your life than your own?*

3.   *What is one act of surrender that you can implement today?*

Contentment will be yours when you surrender to Him; if you are ready, begin by praying this prayer:

Heavenly Father,

I thank you that you know best. Please forgive me for the times when I wanted my will above your Will. Teach me what it means to truly die to self. Help me to give up my plans and desires. Give me the strength to lay it all at the feet of Jesus. Please teach me to truly surrender so my life can be flooded with your contentment. In Jesus' Name I pray, Amen.

Chapter Ten

Situated in Satisfaction

The Apostle Paul wrote some very powerful words when he stated that he had learned to be content whatever the circumstance. He went on to share some examples of how he knew what it was like to be in need and what it was like to have enough. He expressed that he knew what it was like to be hungry and what it was like to have enough to eat.

Philippians 4:10-13 (KJV) *But I rejoiced in the Lord greatly, that now at the last your care of me hath flourished again; wherein ye were also careful, but ye lacked opportunity.*

[11]Not that I speak in respect of want: for I have learned, in whatsoever state I am, therewith to be content.

[12] I know both how to be abased, and I know how to abound: every where and in all things I am instructed both to be full and to be hungry, both to abound and to suffer need.

[13] I can do all things through Christ which strengtheneth me.

Anyone can make a bold statement like that when he/she has everything they need. Anybody can make such claims when he/she has never been through anything. However, that was certainly not the case for Paul. Interestingly enough, Paul was in jail when he wrote this very letter to the church of Philippi. I could be wrong, but I do not think many people are talking about being content in jail. That alone makes him a credible witness for contentment to me.

Paul shared that he had learned the secret to contentment. I truly believe that you and I now know that secret as well. We now understand that our thoughts are powerful and have to be prayerfully guarded. We strongly believe that doubt must go and that we have to trust God no matter what. We recognize that fear will always be present, but we are courageous through Christ Jesus. We do not need any convincing about jealousy; it is evicted and confidence is moving in! Our hardened hearts are being healed right now and we are patiently waiting on God to complete the work. We are resting in the peace of God and we believe that total surrender is the absolute next step.

The secret is out and we have the tools we need to live a life full of contentment! We must be determined to consistently and continually work on the tools shared here in these pages. It will take some getting used to. Take a deep breath and rest assured that this work happens over a lifetime. Before you know it, you will begin to get situated. You will find yourself more relaxed, pulling up a chair, getting cozy with contentment, and situating yourselves right in the midst of satisfaction. You will become so content that the cares of this world will not shake you.

By now, I am sure that you would agree that the journey to contentment requires a great deal of work. Our portion of this journey together is drawing to a close, but I trust that you are encouraged to chase hard after contentment in the days to come and for the rest of your life. The most important thing to remember is that our contentment is found in Christ alone. Remember this when circumstances changes and your days get difficult. As you put these principles into practice, you will not only chase contentment, but you will conquer it and live the fruitful, amazing life God intended for you to live in Christ from the beginning!

1. *Are you able to create a personal definition of contentment?*

2. *What can you do to prepare for your new life of contentment?*

3. *What will life be like for you once you are situated in satisfaction?*

Make the decision to consistently pray this prayer for contentment:

Heavenly Father,

I thank you for guiding me along this journey of contentment. Now, I understand that my contentment is in Christ alone. Lord, please help me to remember that my thoughts are powerful and I have to guard them. Please remove all of the doubt from my life and teach me to trust you no matter what. Help me to be courageous in spite of the fear. Please destroy every bit of jealousy in me and replace it with confidence in you. Touch my hardened heart and heal it more and more each day. Strengthen me as I patiently wait on you to complete the work in me. Hold me as I rest in your peace and totally surrender to Your Will for my life. In Jesus' Name I pray, Amen.

Contentment is maintaining a steady pace until God gives the next direction.

Notes and Scriptural References

Introduction—

- The definition for contentment was found at http://dictionary.reference.com/browse/contentment?s=t.
- Philippians 4:11

Chapter One—

- The article mentioned was found at http://www.rd.com/true-stories/inspiring/hoda-kotb-advice/.
- The National Science Foundation information can be found at http://www.mind-sets.com/html/mindset/thoughts.htm.
- John 16:33
- 2 Corinthians 10:5
- Matthew 18:18
- Philippians 4:8

Chapter Two—

- Some information on the storybook character Eeyore was found at https://en.wikipedia.org/wiki/Eeyore.
- Romans 10:17
- Romans 12:3
- James 1:6
- Hebrews 13:8

Chapter Three—

- Proverbs 3:5-6
- Psalms 139:14

- Isaiah 53:5
- 2 Corinthians 5:7

Chapter Four—

- A list of phobias was found at
  http://psychology.about.com/od/phobias/a/phobialist.htm
- The definition for phobia was found at
  http://dictionary.reference.com/browse/phobia?s=t.
- The survivor story was found at
  http://www.huffingtonpost.com/vanessa-cunningham/3-breast-cancer-survivors_b_6070464.html.
- Deuteronomy 31:14
- Joshua 1:7
- Joshua 1:9
- Joshua 8:1
- Joshua 10:8
- James 2:17
- 2 Timothy 1:7
- Romans 8:15
- 1 John 4:18

Chapter Five—

- James 3:14-16
- Psalms 37:1
- 1 Corinthians 13:4
- Proverbs 14:30
- Romans 12:15
- Psalms 84:11

Chapter Six—

- The definition for heart was found at https://en.wikipedia.org/wiki/Heart and http://dictionary.reference.com/browse/heart?s=t.
- Matthew 15:18
- Ephesians 4:26
- Jeremiah 17:9
- Matthew 6:15
- Psalms 51:10

Chapter Seven—

- Psalms 37:7
- Colossians 3:2

Chapter Eight—

- Philippians 4:6-7
- Matthew 6:27
- Matthew 6:34
- Luke 10:38-42

Chapter Nine—

- The definition of surrender was found at http://dictionary.reference.com/browse/surrender?s=t.
- Psalms 37:4
- Galatians 2:20
- Ephesians 4:22-24
- John 3:30
- Luke 9:23

Chapter Ten—

- Philippians 4:11-13

Author Biography

Shayla L. Hilton is often described as a great listener who is both caring and supportive. She is passionate about lost souls coming into relationship with Jesus Christ. These characteristics help her to reach out and truly connect with people.

Shayla was born and raised in the beautiful state of Virginia, but has since spent the last twelve years in the great state of North Carolina. After graduating from Salem High School in 2003, Shayla began her journey in Greensboro, NC at North Carolina Agricultural and Technical State University. She graduated, four years later, with a bachelor's degree in Elementary Education. She went on to receive two additional advanced degrees. A master's degree in Elementary Education from Elon University and from High Point University, a second master's degree in Educational Leadership.

She is currently an educator by day and a devoted writer by night. She enjoys sharing encouraging words of hope and healing. She chooses to find joy in the mended, but broken pieces of life. Shayla writes from the heart of a woman who has been restored to encourage others not to lose hope, but to passionately pursue contentment through all of life's challenges.

Raised in the church, Shayla's strong biblical foundation was established at Shiloh Baptist Church in Salem, VA under the leadership of Rev. Adrian E. Dowell, Sr. Now, she is an active member of Mount Zion Baptist Church of Greensboro, Inc. under the leadership of Pastor Bryan J. Pierce, Sr.

It is her mission to come alongside women, of all ages, who are lost, broken and hopeless so that they can come into relationship with Jesus Christ, be restored, and live a fruitful and productive life!

Shayla is the only child born to her loving and supportive parents, Steven and Bonita Hilton who still reside in Virginia.

Stay Connected with Shayla

By Mail:	PO Box 8662 Greensboro, NC 27419
By Phone:	(215) 650-7382
Email:	Mshilton85@gmail.com
Blog:	www.HisHavenofHope.blogspot.com
	Shayla Hilton Shayla Hilton @Shay_Lenai @Shay_Lenai
Website:	www.ShaylaHilton.com

CPSIA information can be obtained
at www.ICGtesting.com
Printed in the USA
FFOW01n0150260416
23464FF